Ragtime

9 SELECTIONS FROM THE MUSICAL
Arranged by Dan Coates

T0052549

Ragtime is based on the 1975 best-selling novel of the same name by E. L. Doctorow. The production was written by Terrance McNally (book), Lynn Ahrens (lyrics) and Stephen Flaherty (music). In December 1996, *Ragtime* had its world premiere in Toronto, and a second company followed in Los Angeles in May 1997. On January 18, 1998, it made its Broadway premiere at the newly renovated Ford Center for the Performing Arts where it ran for two years—834 performances—before closing on January 16, 2000. *Ragtime* continues touring with regional theater groups throughout the United States and abroad.

The year is 1906, The Gilded Age, when America promises limitless possibilities of wealth and happiness. The story unfolds in New York with the introduction of characters from three diverse ethnic groups: white upper-middle-class Protestants living pleasant but sheltered lives in a neighborhood with no immigrants or people of color; African-Americans seeking equality, opportunity and respect; and Eastern European Jewish immigrants who sailed to America in search of a better life. *Ragtime* is about individuals from those three groups who cross their cultural, ethnic and socioeconomic barriers, and whose lives come together in the most unforeseen ways. Additionally, the cast includes both fictional characters and historical figures such as Booker T. Washington, Harry Houdini and Evelyn Nesbit, whose real-life circumstances are interwoven throughout the story. Emotions run the whole gamut—longing, love, compassion, frustration, disillusionment, and anger that escalates into violence. The story, however, ends very optimistically with the promise of a brighter future and "New Music" for all.

Ragtime received 12 Tony Award nominations, winning Best Featured Actress (Audra McDonald), Best Original Score (Ahrens and Flaherty), Best Book of a Musical (McNally) and Best Orchestrations (William David Brohn). A poignant and touching musical drama about life at the turn of the 20th century, *Ragtime* is truly one of **Broadway's Best**!

Contents

Ragtime

Lyrics by Lynn Ahrens
Music by Stephen Flaherty
Arranged by Dan Coates

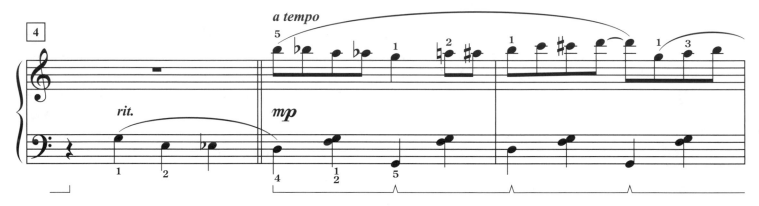

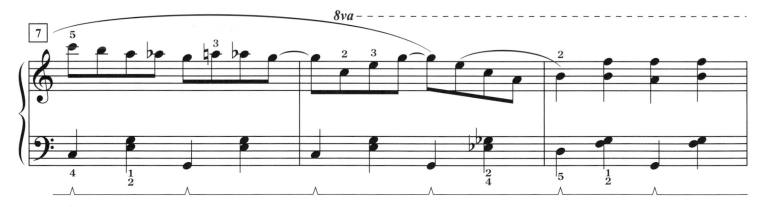

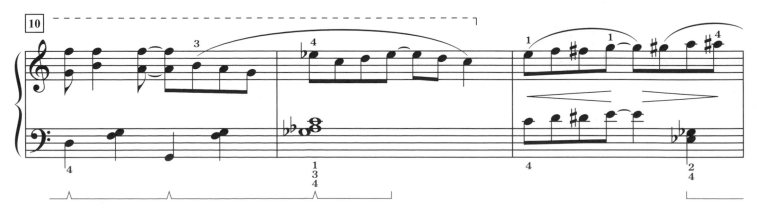

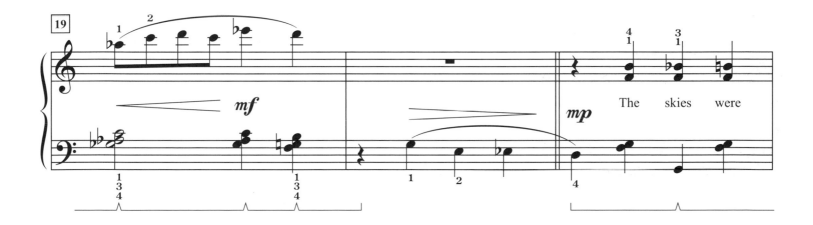

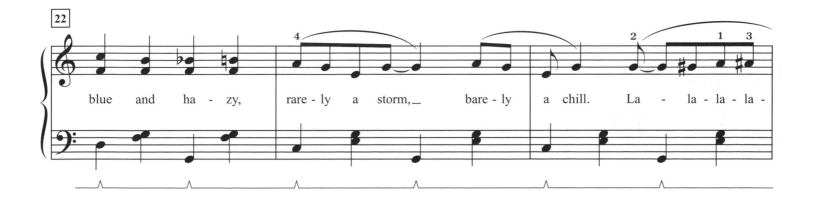

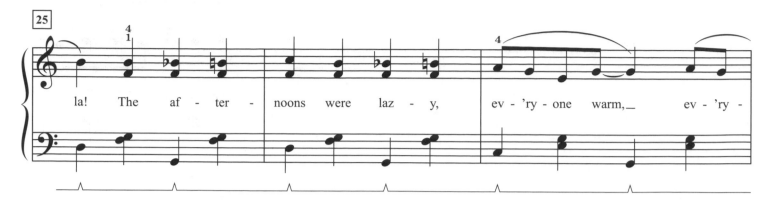

la! The af - ter - noons were laz - y, ev - 'ry - one warm,__ ev - 'ry -

thing still. La - la - la - la - la! And there was dis - tant mu - sic,

cresc.

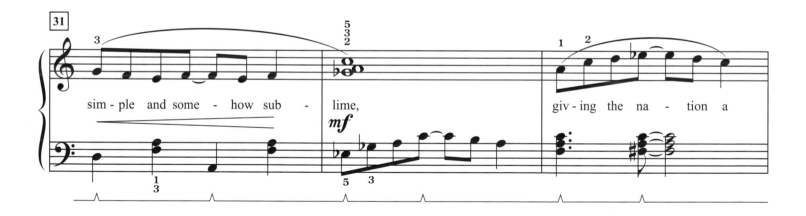

sim - ple and some - how sub - lime,

mf

giv - ing the na - tion a

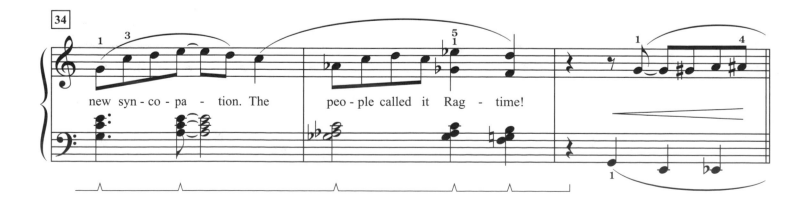

new syn - co - pa - tion. The peo - ple called it Rag - time!

And there was dis - tant mu - sic, skip - ping a beat,___ sing - ing

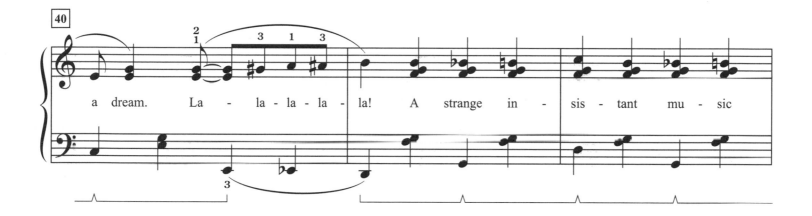

a dream. La - la - la - la - la! A strange in - sis - tant mu - sic

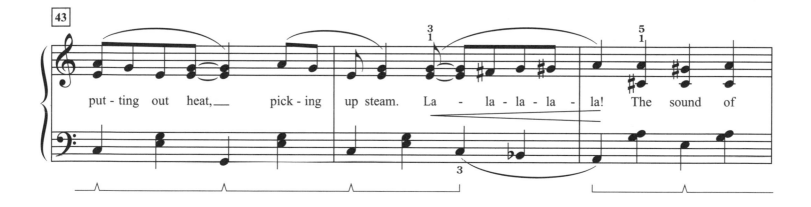

put - ting out heat,___ pick - ing up steam. La - la - la - la - la! The sound of

dis - tant thun - der sud - den - ly start - ing to climb...___

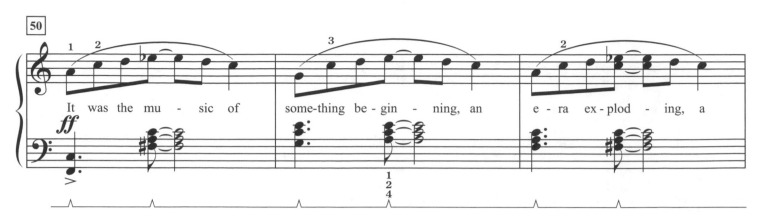

It was the mu - sic of   some-thing be - gin - ning, an   e - ra ex - plod - ing, a

cen - tu - ry spin - ning in   rich - es and rags__ and in   rhy - thm and rhyme.__   The

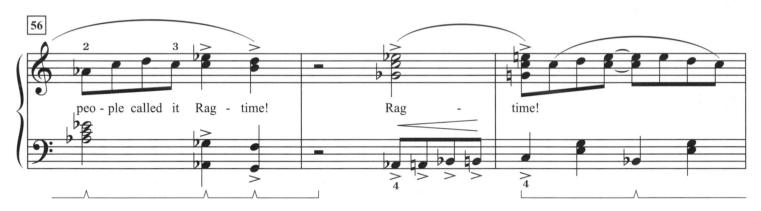

peo - ple called it Rag - time!   Rag -   time!

Rag -   time!   Rag -

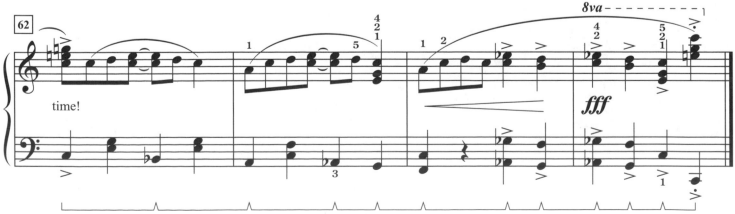

time!

New Music

Lyrics by Lynn Ahrens
Music by Stephen Flaherty
Arranged by Dan Coates

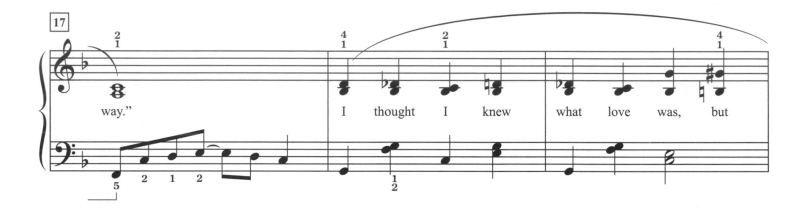

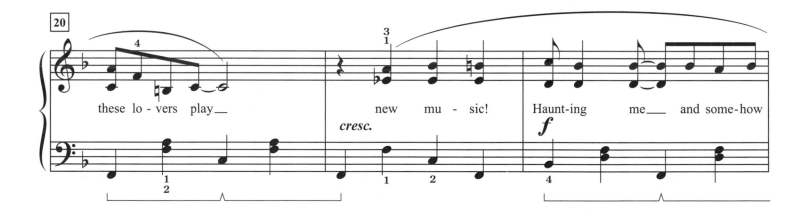

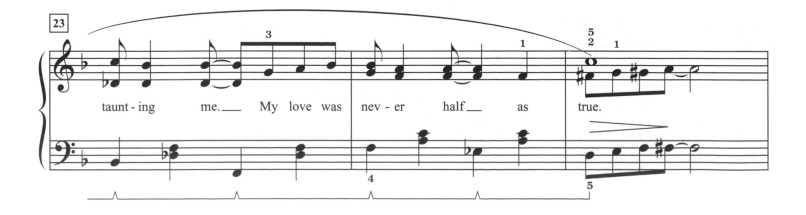

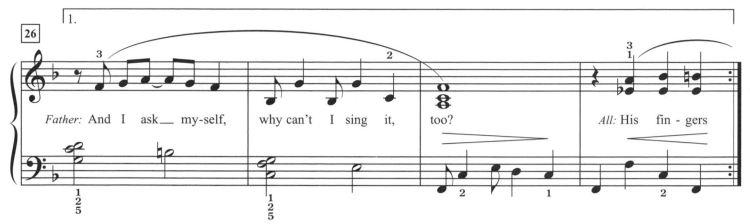

Father: And I ask__ my-self, why can't I sing it, too? All: His fin - gers

Coalhouse: Sa - rah, my life__ had changed. Sa - rah, you've got__ to see. Sa - rah, we've got__ a son.

Sa - rah, come down__ to me. *poco rall.* *mp* *a tempo* *cresc. poco a poco*

Sarah: You and your mu - sic, sing - ing deep__ in me,

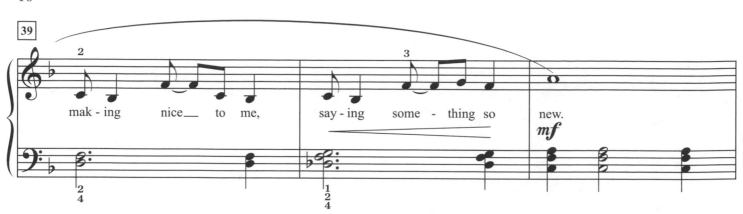

mak - ing   nice___   to   me,   say - ing   some - thing   so   new.

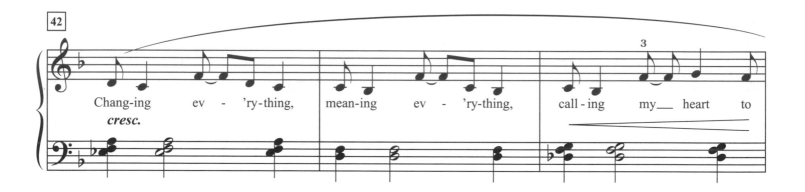

Chang - ing   ev - 'ry - thing,   mean - ing   ev - 'ry - thing,   call - ing   my___   heart   to

cresc.

you...   Play   that   mel - o - dy,   your   sweet   mel - o - dy,   call - ing   my___ heart   to

f   *rall.*

you!

ff

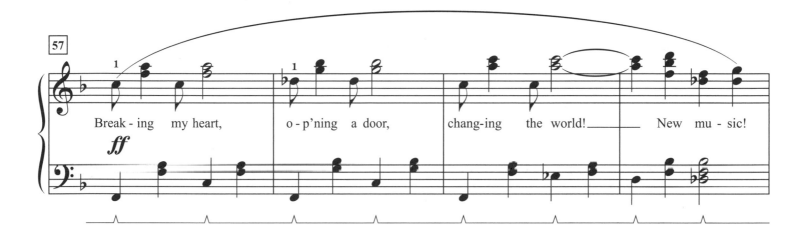

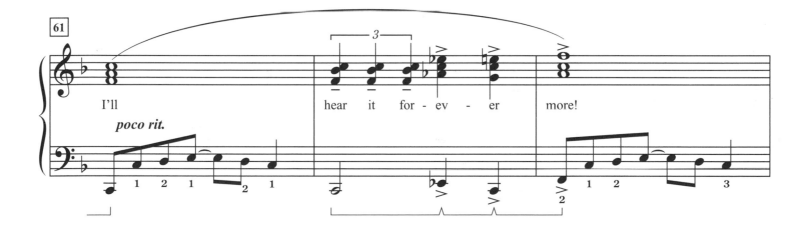

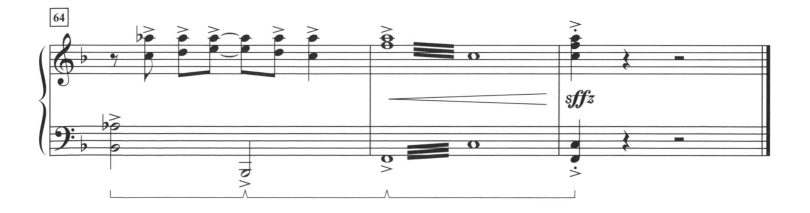

Goodbye, My Love

Lyrics by Lynn Ahrens
Music by Stephen Flaherty
Arranged by Dan Coates

You need to know I'll be there at the win -

dow_____ while you go your way._____

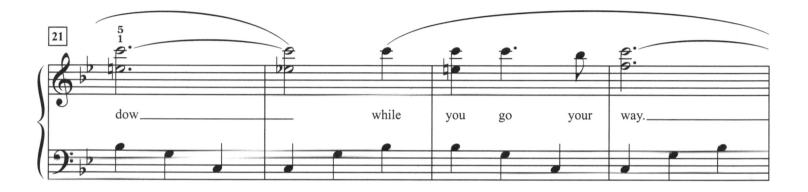

_____ I ac - cept that. But

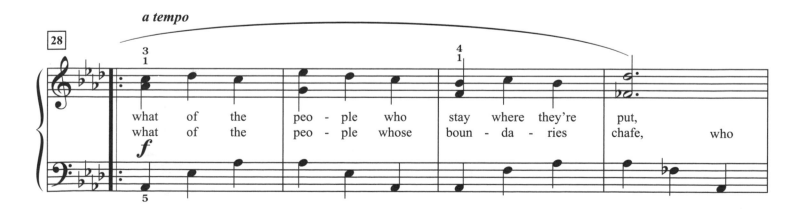

what of the peo - ple who stay where they're put,
what of the peo - ple whose boun - da - ries chafe, who

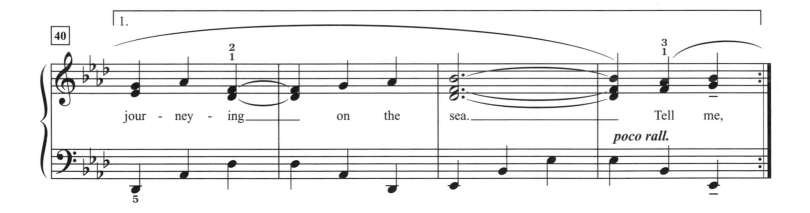

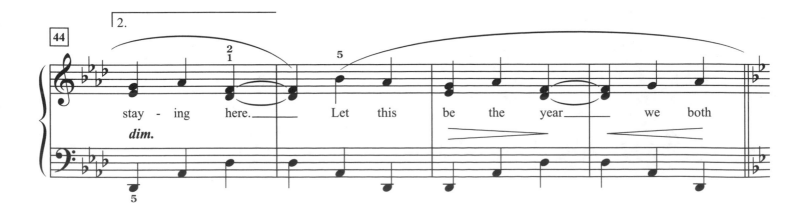

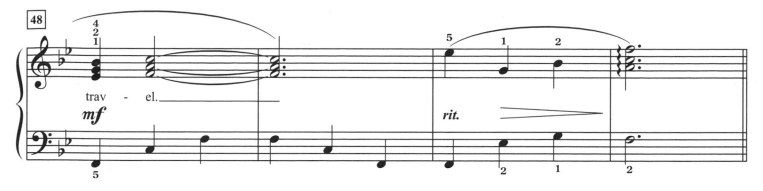

trav - el.

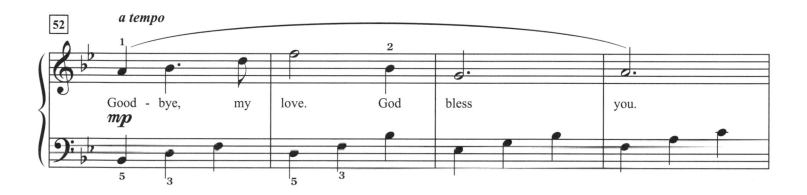

Good - bye, my love. God bless you.

Some - how I know I'll be jour - ney - ing too.

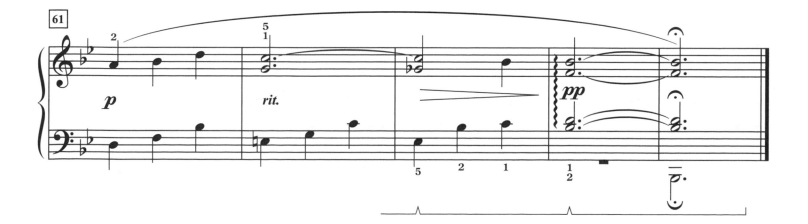

Your Daddy's Son

Lyrics by Lynn Ahrens
Music by Stephen Flaherty
Arranged by Dan Coates

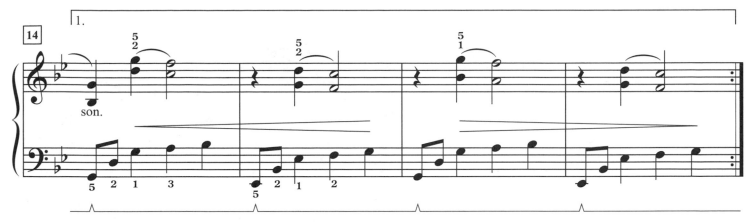

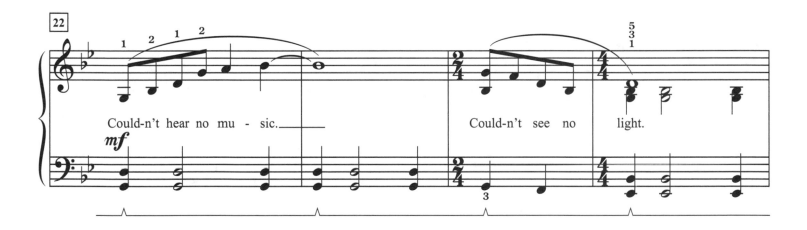

Tears with-out no com - fort, screams with-out no sound.

On - ly dark-ness and pain, the an - ger and pain, the blood and the pain! I

bur - ied my heart in the ground! In the ground,

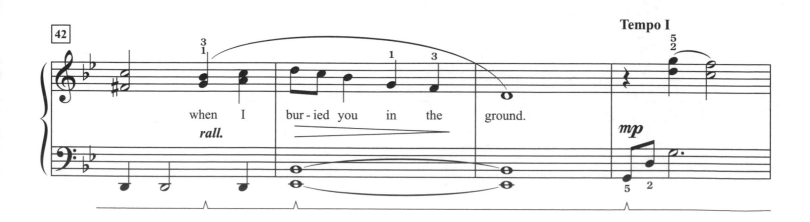

when I bur - ied you in the ground.

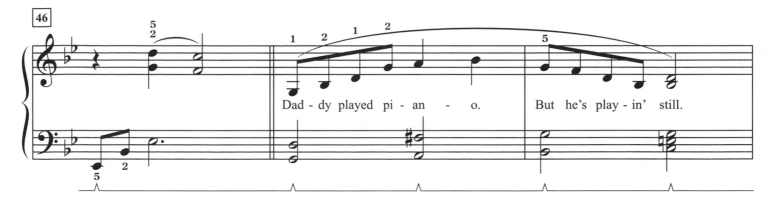

Dad - dy played pi - an - o. But he's play - in' still.

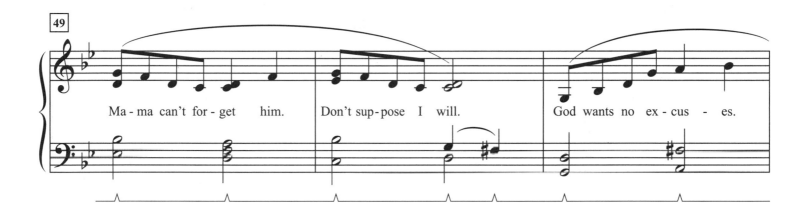

Ma - ma can't for - get him. Don't sup - pose I will. God wants no ex - cus - es.

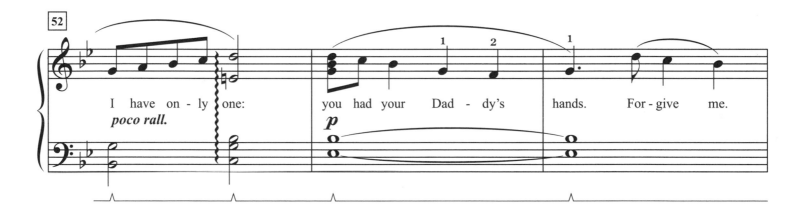

I have on - ly one: you had your Dad - dy's hands. For - give me.

poco rall. *p*

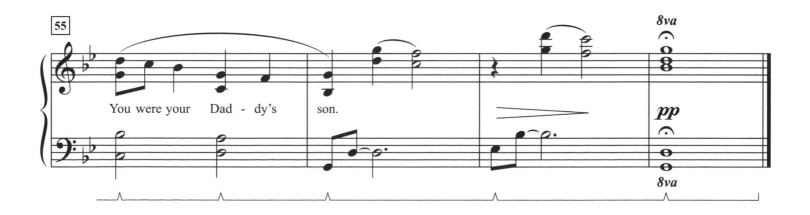

You were your Dad - dy's son.

8va *pp* *8va*

Wheels of a Dream

Lyrics by Lynn Ahrens
Music by Stephen Flaherty
Arranged by Dan Coates

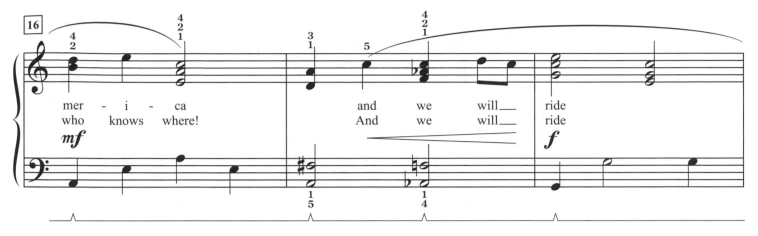

mer - i - ca   and we will___ ride
who knows where!   And we will___ ride

mf   *f*

on the wheels   of a dream.
on the wheels   of a

decresc.   *mf*

We'll go down___   dream.

mf legato

a tempo

rit. e dim.   *f*   *cresc. poco a poco*

Be - yond that road, be - yond this

life - time, this time full of hope

will al - ways gleam with the pro - mise of

hap - pi - ness and the free - dom he'll live to know.

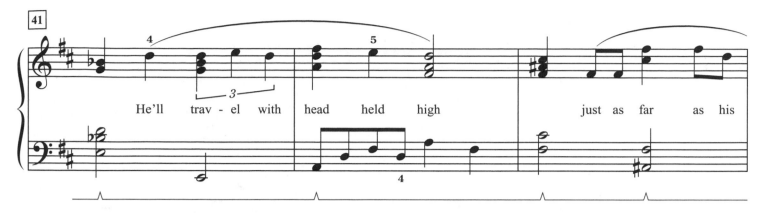

He'll trav - el with head held high   just as far as his

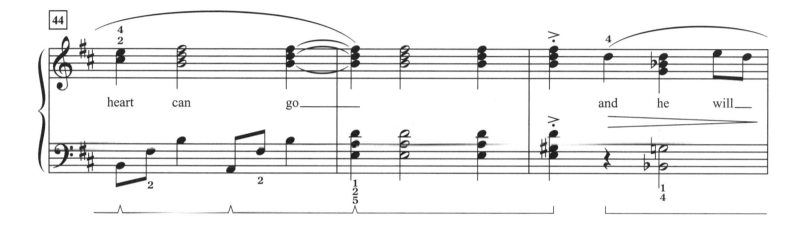

heart can go   and he will

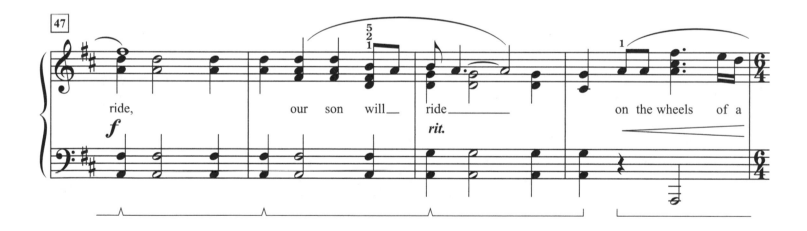

ride,   our son will ride   on the wheels of a

Maestoso

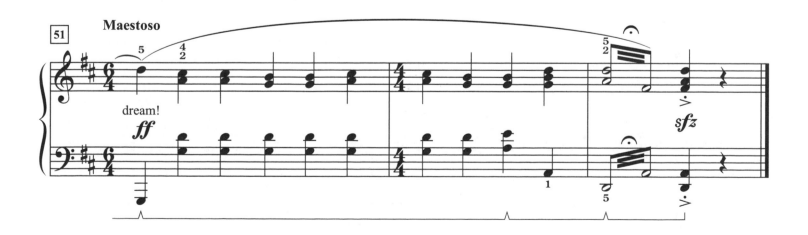

dream!

Our Children

Lyrics by Lynn Ahrens
Music by Stephen Flaherty
Arranged by Dan Coates

laugh.
fair,

She has nev - er
and the oth - er

laughed like this.
lithe and dark.

Ev - 'ry wak - ing
So - lemn joy and

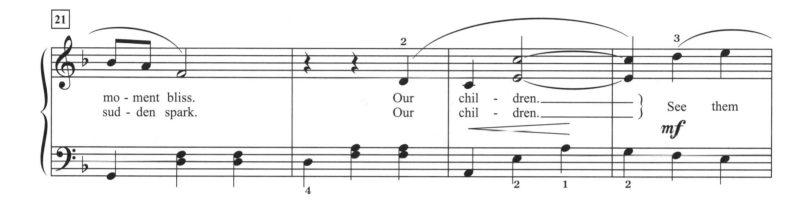

mo - ment bliss.
sud - den spark.

Our
Our

chil - dren.
chil - dren.

See them
mf

run - ning down the beach.

Chil - dren run

so   fast

toward   the

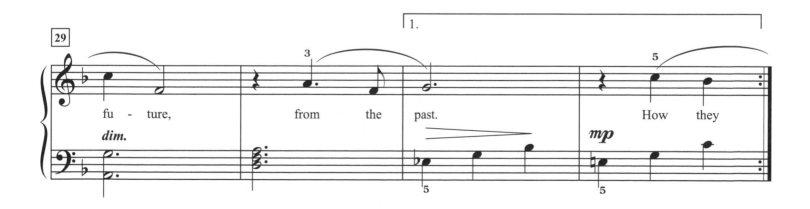

fu - ture,
dim.

from   the   past.

How   they
mp

26

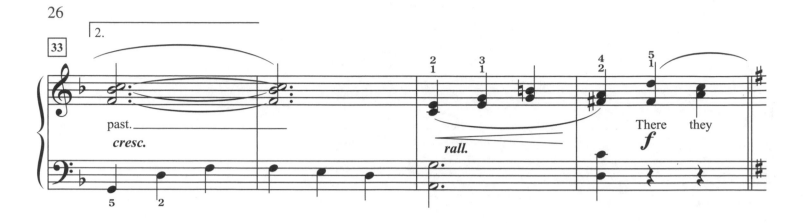

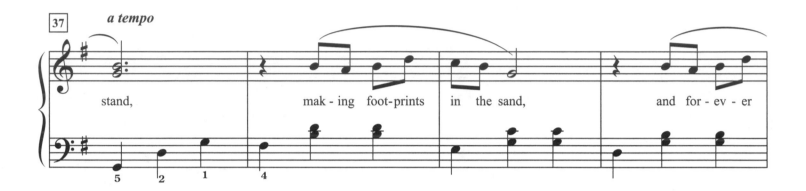

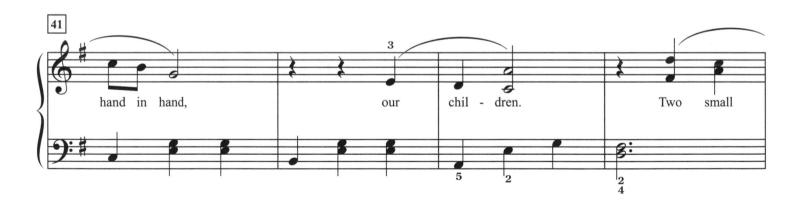

one like_____ you._____

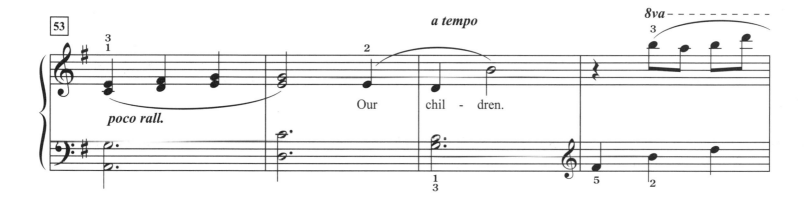

poco rall. Our chil - dren.

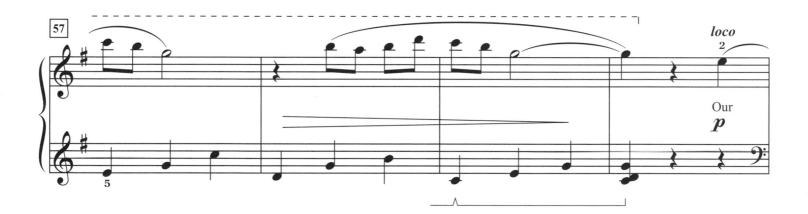

Our

chil - dren._____
rit.

Back to Before

Lyrics by Lynn Ahrens
Music by Stephen Flaherty
Arranged by Dan Coates

bend - ing.
chant - ed.

Our lit - tle road with nev - er a
If I had dreams, then I let you
cresc.

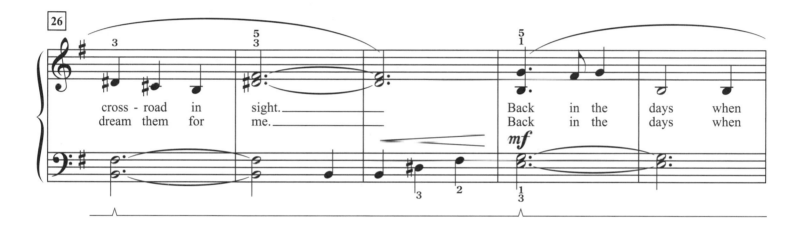

cross - road in sight.
dream them for me.
mf

Back in the days when
Back in the days when

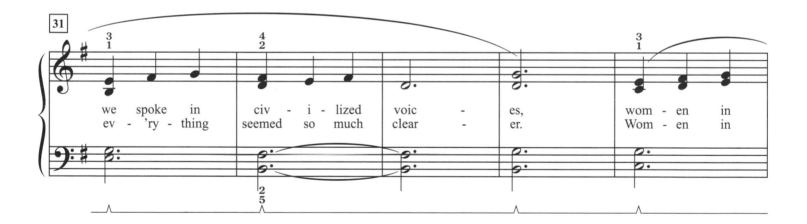

we spoke in civ - i - lized voic - es,
ev - 'ry - thing seemed so much clear - er.

wom - en in
Wom - en in

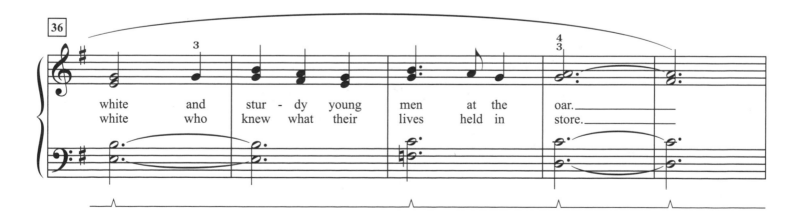

white and stur - dy young men at the oar.
white who knew what their lives held in store.

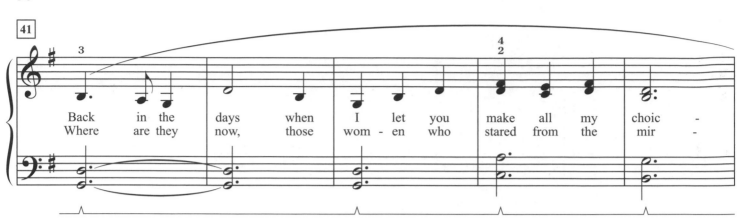

Back in the days when I let you make all my choic-
Where are they now, when those wom - en who stared from the mir -

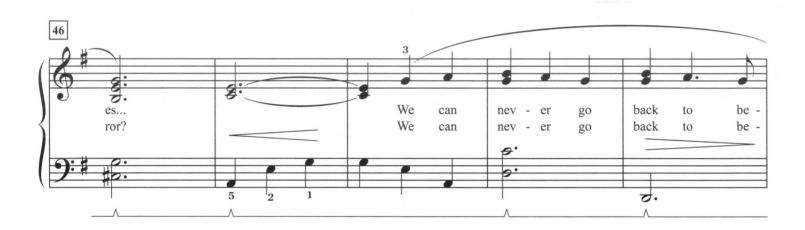

es... We can nev - er go back to be -
ror? We can nev - er go back to be -

1.

fore.
mp

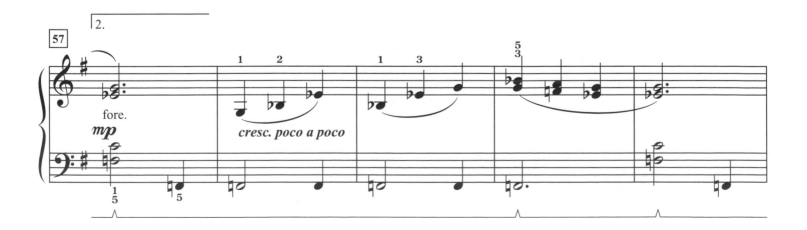

2.

fore.
mp
cresc. poco a poco

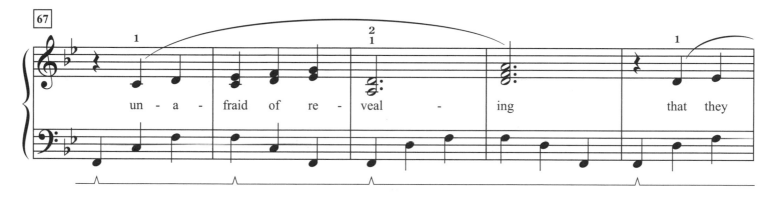

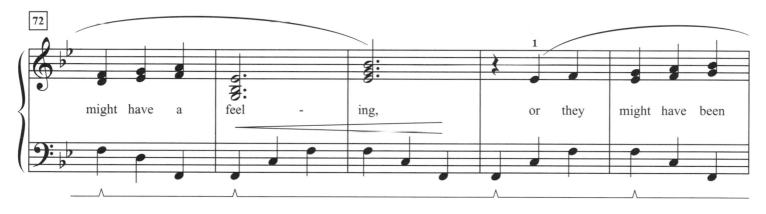

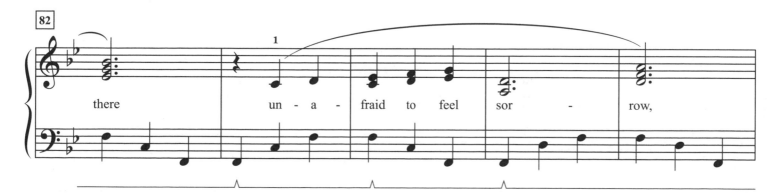

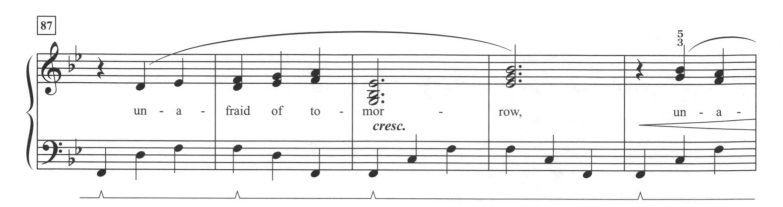

un - a - fraid of to - mor - row,   un - a -

cresc.

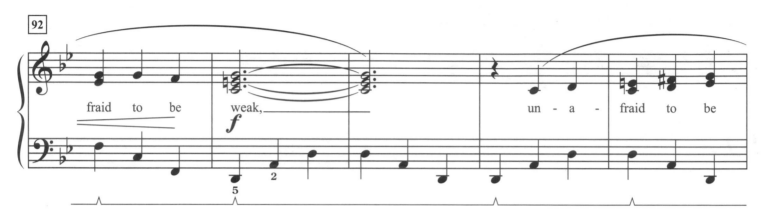

fraid to be   weak, _____   un - a - fraid to be

f

strong.   *mf*
poco rall.

a tempo

There was a   time   when   you were the   per - son in   mo -

f

tion.   I was your   wife.   It   nev - er oc - curred to   want

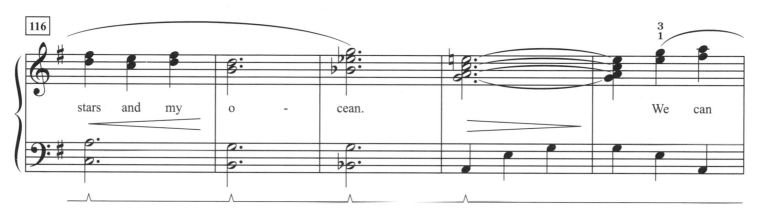

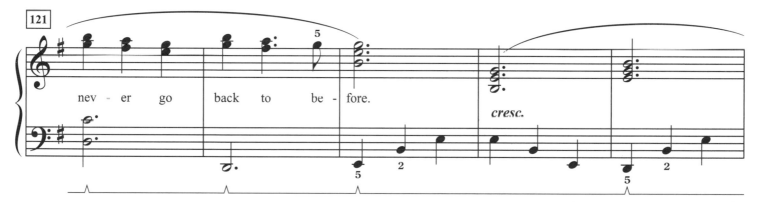

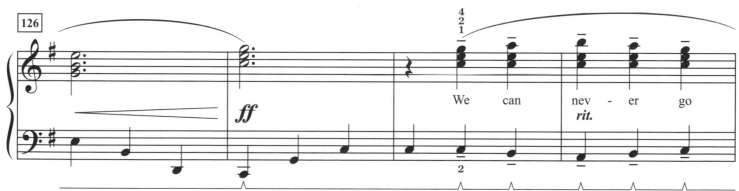

'Till We Reach That Day

Lyrics by Lynn Ahrens
Music by Stephen Flaherty
Arranged by Dan Coates

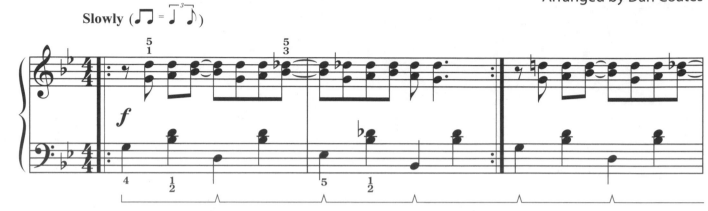

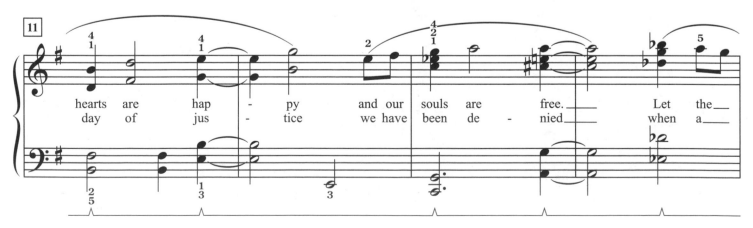

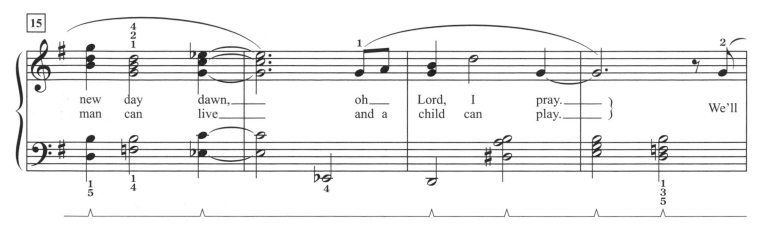

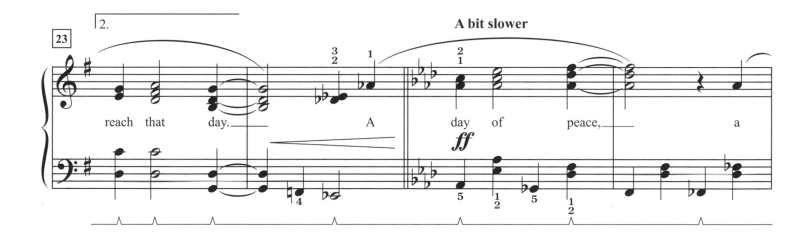

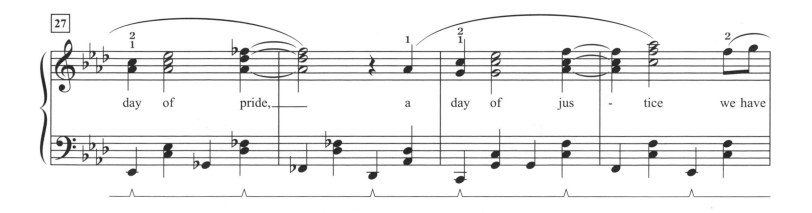

been de - nied. Let the new day dawn. Oh___

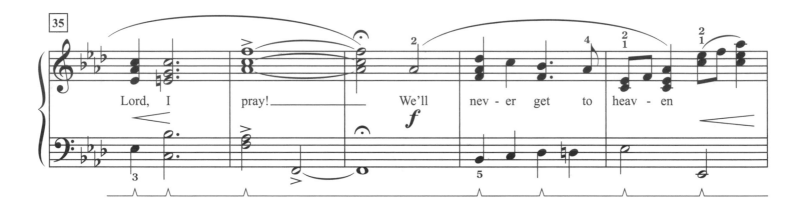

Lord, I pray!___ We'll nev - er get to heav - en

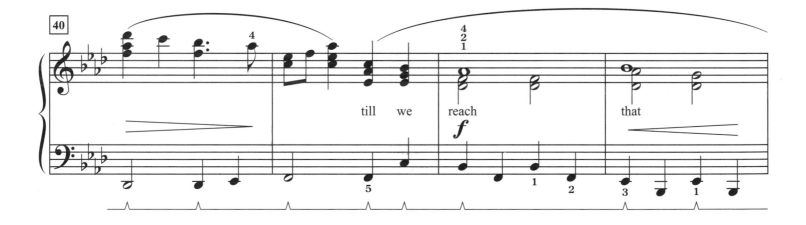

till we reach that

day!

Make Them Hear You

Lyrics by Lynn Ahrens
Music by Stephen Flaherty
Arranged by Dan Coates

hear you. Your sword can be a ser-mon of the pow-er of the pen. Teach

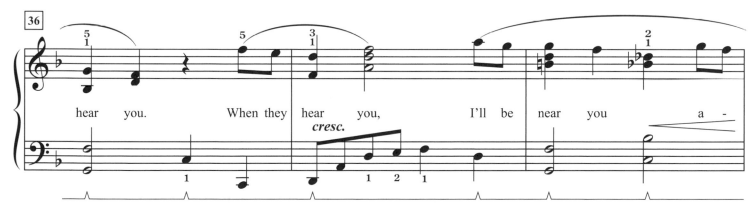

ev-'ry child to raise his voice and then, my bro-thers, then will

rall.

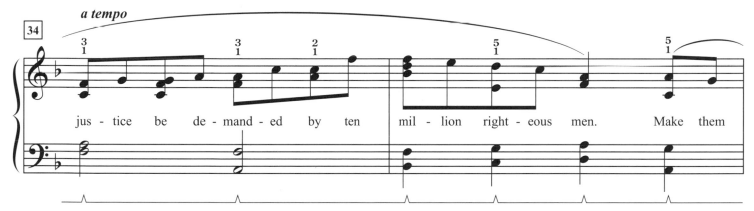

a tempo

jus-tice be de-mand-ed by ten mil-lion right-eous men. Make them

hear you. When they hear you, I'll be near you a-

cresc.

gain.

ff

sfz

8va